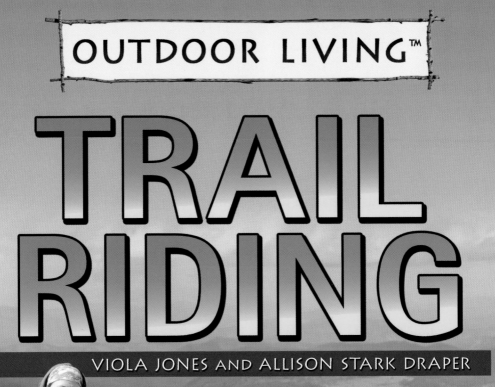

OUTDOOR LIVING™

TRAIL RIDING

VIOLA JONES AND ALLISON STARK DRAPER

ROSEN
PUBLISHING

NEW YORK

Published in 2016 by The Rosen Publishing Group, Inc.
29 East 21st Street, New York, NY 10010

First Edition

Library of Congress Cataloging-in-Publication Data

Jones, Viola.
 Trail riding / Viola Jones and Allison Stark Draper. -- First edition.
      pages cm. -- (Outdoor living)
 Includes index.
 Audience: Grades 7 to 12.
 ISBN 978-1-4994-6239-5 (library bound)
 1. Trail riding--Juvenile literature. I. Draper, Allison Stark. II. Title.
 SF309.28.J66 2015
 798.2'3--dc23
                        2015024901

Manufactured in China

CONTENTS

INTRODUCTION

Do you love the outdoors? Would you rather be outside, enjoying the beauty of nature, even if your friends want to stay inside watching TV or talking on the phone? If hiking, cross-country skiing, or similar activities are up your alley, consider taking up trail riding as well.

Trail riding is a great way to enjoy scenery from a unique perspective—on horseback. From high above the trail you will see things you might not notice from the ground. And you'll experience this invigorating activity with a friend: a majestic horse. Imagine waking at dawn to ride through fields of mist, trotting on a beach at sunset, galloping through the snow on a clear winter day, or cantering along a riverbed to enjoy fall foliage.

If you've never even set foot near a horse, do not be intimidated. This resource will teach you about the different breeds of horses, prepare you for selecting an appropriate horse to ride, and give you tips on acclimating to the horse and properly caring for him or her. You will learn how to ride and specifically how to ride safely on a trail.

If you are already familiar with horses, then you're one step ahead of the game. You might not need to learn the basics of how to ride, but that doesn't mean you're ready to hit the trail just yet. This resource will be invaluable in outlining the tips and procedures specific to trail riding, how best to enjoy it, and potential hazards to watch out for.

Trail riding combines horseback riding with nature appreciation. If you love animals and the rugged outdoors, this may be the activity for you.

Either way, you are about to discover a new and exciting activity that combines an appreciation of the wilderness with the connection to another living creature. Hold on to your reins!

CHAPTER 1

THE HORSE'S LONG HISTORY

Agrazing version of the modern horse appeared about ten to fifteen million years ago. But the horse has been evolving for at least fifty million years. We know this because a fossil of *Hyracotherium*, the horse's earliest-known ancestor, has been discovered. *Hyracotherium* was about the size of a dog and roamed the forests and swamps of North America. Over time, and with environmental changes, this creature adapted to grassy open plains, growing long legs and increasing in size.

The "true," or one-toed, horse (*Equus*) that we know today probably originated in North and Central America. At one time, Alaska and Russia were still connected by a land bridge. Some of these original horses crossed this land bridge into Asia and traveled across to Europe and down into Africa. Horses then became extinct on the American continents but thrived in Europe, Asia, and Africa. *Equus* is therefore the source of all modern horses all over the world. It is also the source of such horse relatives as the donkey and the zebra.

HORSES AND HUMANS

Humans have been riding horses for almost five thousand years. Historically, horses have provided people with transportation, companionship, meat, and milk. They have carried hunters after large and fast game. They have carried warriors into battle. They have also represented material wealth. In times when money was not in common use, owning horses showed that a person was rich and important.

Unearthed in Pompeii, Italy, this horse skeleton was likely buried in ash during the eruption of Mount Vesuvius in the year 79.

Cave paintings from the Stone Age suggest that very early peoples used a harness or collar to control their horses. The hunters who stalked wild horse herds for meat discovered that horses could be tamed. Some of these nomadic peoples traveled great distances with their horses. They introduced the use of horses to people they met and allowed their horses to interbreed with wild horses during their journeys. By 3000 BC, both the nomadic peoples of Asiatic Russia and the peoples of ancient Assyria and Babylonia were keeping horses, riding horses, and using horses to pull and carry heavy loads.

One important early use of the horse was in war. The Egyptians used horses to pull their weapon-filled chariots into battle. The Persians, who were excellent riders, rode into battle and found horses to be a great advantage. A mounted warrior is both taller and more agile than a charioteer. By 500 BC, the Persians had developed cavalry squadrons of horses powerful enough to carry riders wearing heavy armor. The ancient Greeks were also strong riders and

This Spanish mosaic from the third century depicts a carriage race powered by horses.

fought on horseback like their mythical centaurs.

The Romans used hundreds of thousands of horses in their armies. They also used horses in the construction of their temples, monuments, and roads. They brought horses from southern to northern Europe and far to the east. They are responsible for the interbreeding that created such breeds as the Dales and Fell ponies of England. In the eighth century, the Moors invaded Europe. They brought thousands of barb and Arabian horses into Spain. In the sixteenth century, the Spanish invaded America and brought their Spanish barbs across the Atlantic Ocean by ship. Millions of years after its journey across the Alaskan land bridge, the horse had finally returned to its birthplace in North America.

HORSES IN AMERICA

The history of the American frontier is all about courage and stamina. The Western horse, who has both, had a lot to do with building the West. Bred to handle cattle, the Western horse is fast enough to outrun a wild bull. It is enduring enough to gallop all day long carrying a two-hundred-pound man and one hundred pounds of rope. It is nimble enough to stop dead from a gallop and strong enough to throw its weight against that of an uncooperative cow. It is smart and brave enough to herd or help lasso a steer. A Western horse also has to be reliable and obedient because on foot a cowboy has no protection from the long horns of wild cattle.

The early Californian cattle ranchers imported Spanish horses called barbs. The barb breed is known for its spirit and endurance. Barbs came originally from the Barbary region of North Africa and

COLORS AND MARKINGS

Horses come in a wide range of colors and markings. Like many animals, horses were originally the same color as their environments and therefore less visible to predators. This is called camouflage. Many early horses were dun, which is a yellow-gray color that made them hard to see on grassy plains.

Today most horse colors have to do with breeding and human desires. The color of a horse is the color of its coat. Its markings are its points (mane, tail, and lower legs) and face. Common horse colors include black, bay (reddish brown or red with black points), liver chestnut (brown), chestnut (red), gray, palomino (gold with white points), and paint or pinto (two-colored). Common facial markings include stripes, stars, and blazes.

were used widely on the Spanish plains, both areas of the world that resemble parts of the American West.

The barb is the traditional horse of the Bedouin nomads of the North African deserts. Barbs were brought to Spain by the Moors, and there the breed mixed with the native Spanish horses to create the Spanish barb. Usually bay (reddish brown with a black mane and tail), brown, chestnut, black, or gray, the barb stands fourteen to fifteen hands high, which means four feet eight inches or five feet at the shoulder. A "hand" is four inches, or the width of the average human palm. Typically, the barb has a long, straight head; large, forward-set eyes; a strong, erect neck; a short, compact body; a low-set tail; and long, sleek legs. It is courageous, quick-tempered, surefooted, and very tough.

Some of the barbs the ranchers brought to America escaped and ran wild on the North American plains. Their offspring adapted to the tough conditions of the plains and became the wild mustangs of the West. These horses were adopted by the Native American tribes of the plains. When English-speaking settlers arrived in the West, they discovered that mustangs were ideal for cattle ranching. A strong mustang could carry its rider eighty to one hundred miles

Mustangs are the wild horses of the American West. Beautiful, fast, and strong, they were used by Native Americans and American settlers on the frontier.

in a day.

The American horse was born in all colors. Spotted Appaloosas, two-toned pintos, and silver-maned golden palominos are all American breeds descended from the original mustangs. Today, Western horses fall into three main categories: the dependable trail horse, the nimble ranch horse, and the beautiful show horse. Many Western horses have some quarter horse blood. Quarter horses trace their lineage back to early crossbreeding between the tough Spanish cow horse and the faster, more elegant English thoroughbred. Known as "America's horse," the quarter horse is a major competitor in such Western events as racing and rodeo.

Now that you understand the history of the modern horse, you'll need to think about choosing the horse you'll ride. There are several factors to consider, but you are one step closer to getting out on the trail!

CHAPTER 2

HORSE BREEDS

Before you go out on the trail, you'll need something that is essential to trail riding: a horse. There are many types of horses to choose from, and you'll need the help of an expert to help you select one. Talk to a person at a stable for guidance about which horse is right for you.

Every horse is different in its skills, strengths, and temperament. A horse will not be right for you simply because you fall in love with it. When you choose the right horse and ride it on trails or competitive courses, you will love its ability to support you and become your close working partner on the trail.

You should think about temperament as well as ability. Perhaps you want to start with a pony. Maybe you want a jumper. Perhaps you want a docile, gentle horse, or a horse that will be comfortable on dry or rocky terrain. Whatever you decide, you must like a horse's personality. The breed characteristics that affect personality are a good starting point for your search.

An important thing to consider when choosing a horse is what breed you think matches your needs. There is amazing variety in horse breeds. What makes a breed distinctive? Well, some ancient breeds, like the Arabian, were bred for their beauty, intelligence, and endurance. Other breeds, like the huge Clydesdales (which you might recognize as the horses in the Budweiser commercials) were bred for their great strength. Then there are breeds that look unique, such as Appaloosas, which are special because of their spotted markings. Read on to learn about just a few of the many breeds of horses there are in the world.

THE OLDEST PUREBRED: THE ARABIAN

The Arabian is the oldest purebred horse in the world. There are eight-thousand-year-old rock paintings of horses in northern Africa that look like today's Arabian. The most famous Arabians are those of the Bedouin Arabs. The ancient Bedouins needed horses that could survive in their hot, dry desert homeland. They also wanted horses beautiful enough to demonstrate their wealth and power. For more than two thousand years, they have bred their bravest and strongest mares with their most intelligent and beautiful stallions. They are very careful never to breed one of their horses with a horse whose blood is not pure Arabian.

When an Arabian does breed with another horse, its offspring always have some Arabian qualities. These include stamina, high-spiritedness, and shape. This makes the Arabian a very popular breeding horse. It has been crossed with almost every other kind

Among their other outstanding qualities, Arabians are excellent trail horses. Their intelligence and stamina make them ideal companions on the trail.

of horse in the world. The Arabian is also a good riding horse. It is a particularly good horse for trail riding because of its endurance. The Arabian is usually chestnut, bay, or gray. It stands between fourteen and fifteen hands, or around five feet at the shoulder. It has a small head with a dished face and large, wide-set eyes; an arched neck; short back; and long, finely boned legs.

THE WILD MUSTANG

The mustang is the wild horse of North America. The descendant of the Spanish settlers' horses, it has both barb and Arabian blood.

In the three hundred years that mustangs ran wild on the western plains, they evolved into tough, smart, independent horses. Many of the best mustangs were caught by American Indians and later by cowboys and used as riding horses.

The mustang was crossed with larger breeds to produce larger workhorses for pulling wagons and stagecoaches. Eventually, it was crossed with the thoroughbred. The offspring of the mustang and the thoroughbred is one of the most important American breeds, the quarter horse. There is also mustang blood in Appaloosas, palominos, and pintos. There are not many wild mustangs left. Today they are considered endangered and are protected by law. Mustangs come in all colors. They stand fourteen to fifteen hands, or around five feet high, at the shoulder. They are lightweight with strong legs. They are nimble and hardy and can be headstrong. Today they are used as ranch horses and for recreational and endurance riding.

THE WORLD'S RACEHORSE: THE THOROUGHBRED

The thoroughbred is the fastest horse in the world. It is also the most valuable. Developed in the 1700s, the thoroughbred is the child of the fastest British mares and Arabian, barb, and Turk stallions. All serious racing thoroughbreds are the descendants of three Arabian stallions: the Byerley Turk, the Darley Arabian—the great-grandfather of Eclipse, one of the most famous racehorses of all time—and the Godolphin Arabian.

The thoroughbred comes in most solid colors and stands tall at 14.2 to 17.2 hands, or around five feet six inches at the shoulder.

A PONY IS NOT A BABY HORSE!

If you know a little about the horse world, you might know that, in general, horses are big and ponies are little. What you may not know is that ponies do not grow up to be horses. A pony compared to a horse is like a terrier compared to a German shepherd. Ponies are not baby horses, but fully grown, pint-sized breeds of the species of the modern horse, *Equus*. The word for baby horse is "foal." If a foal is a boy, he is a colt, and if she is a girl, she is a filly.

It has an elegant head, a long arched neck, long back, long legs, a deep chest, and muscular hindquarters. It is bold and spirited but not headstrong or stubborn. It has a long, smooth stride and is a perfect riding horse.

THE TINY SHETLAND PONY

Named for its homeland, the Shetland Islands of northern Scotland, the Shetland pony is one of the smallest horses in the world. It is also one of the strongest for its size. In the 1800s, this combination of strength and small size made it very useful as a workhorse in the coal mines. Its size also makes it a good pony for young riders. It is lively and smart and performs well in shows and competitions. Shetlands do tend to have minds of their own, so their riders need to be confident and assertive. Otherwise, a Shetland pony can be

Their tiny size makes Shetland ponies ideal for children to ride, but they can be headstrong.

headstrong and hard to control.

The tiny Shetland is only about 10.2 hands, or three feet six inches at the shoulder. It is usually brown, black, bay, chestnut, gray, or two-colored. It has a small head, a compact, thickset body, and short legs with "feathers," or tufts of hair, on them.

THE PRETTY WELSH PONY

The original Welsh mountain pony is an ancient breed. It existed as long ago as the Roman invasion of England. After thousands of years in the craggy Welsh mountains, the Welsh pony is surefooted and quick, as well as a good jumper. It is also brave, gentle, and intelligent. Welsh ponies are excellent for both beginners and experienced riders.

The modern Welsh pony is considered one of the prettiest ponies and owes its beautiful dished face to the fact that it has some Arabian blood. Welsh ponies come in most colors. They are not higher than twelve hands, or four feet, at the shoulder. They have small heads, high-set tails, and elegant short legs.

Once you have selected a horse, it is time to become acquainted with it. You might love it right away, but it may not feel the same about you. Read on to learn more about your horse.

CHAPTER 3

EXPLORING YOUR HORSE

Getting to know your horse is something you should do right away. Spend some time with it and see how it reacts to you. Can you tell its personality? Think about how you would adapt differently to a gentle horse or a quick-tempered horse.

A THINKING CREATURE

People are often skeptical of the idea that horses are intelligent creatures with definite personalities. There is no question that horses think. Just like people, some of them are smarter than others. In fact, some horses are clever enough to make your life impossible. There are horses that can figure out how to let themselves out of any stall, stable, barn, or paddock. Some of them will wait until you aren't paying attention and let out not only themselves but all of their stable mates.

Horses are intelligent creatures with distinct personalities. It is worth taking the time to get to know your horse before you embark on a trail ride.

As animals in the wild, horses are herd members. They depend upon the leadership and intelligence of a dominant member, usually a stallion, to make survival decisions. There are numerous legends about wild herds that were able to avoid capture by staying one step ahead of their human pursuers. Most of the members of these herds were just following the orders of the lead stallion. And they preferred it that way, which is why the human-horse relationship is usually so productive. If a rider is smart, sensible, and trustworthy, a horse will work hard, follow orders, and give its all for food, protection, and love.

AN UNUSUAL WAY OF SLEEPING

Horses need only about four hours of sleep a day. In the wild, they usually sleep standing up so that they can gallop out of sudden danger. They do this by locking their front legs and allowing their weight to rest on their breastbone. When a horse is sleeping standing up, it can rest a rear leg but not a foreleg. This is why you sometimes see horses dozing with one cocked hind leg. Horses do have to lie down in order to experience the truly deep sleep in which they probably dream, just as humans do.

HOW TO TREAT YOUR HORSE

Horses, just like humans, learn by association. This means that if your command to walk west out of the stable yard always leads to a pleasant trail ride and something your horse particularly enjoys, like a swim, your horse will love to turn west. On the other hand, if your appearance with a blue halter always leads to a trip in the van to the vet and a shot, your horse will come to hate the blue halter. For this reason, it is smart to combine even the most unpleasant chores with something desirable, like a special treat. Remember when you were a kid and your doctor gave you a lollipop after your examination? Treat your horse the same way. Otherwise your horse may develop "irrational" reactions, like refusing to move at the sight of something blue, that are actually perfectly sensible responses.

Reward your horse with a special treat when undertaking unpleasant chores like going to the vet for a shot.

When you train your horse with voice commands, use short, simple sounds. Horses remember specific commands best if they are no more than one to three syllables long. Horses are very sensitive to the tone of your voice. It will help your horse to understand and obey you if you always pronounce your commands in the same way. Horses are also sensitive to the emotions in your voice, like fear, urgency, or praise. They tend to enjoy streams of words spoken in pleasant or soothing tones.

Horses are large animals, and their eyes are located way at the front of their bodies. As a result, they are very sensitive to sudden touches or noises near parts of themselves that they cannot see. Always talk soothingly to a horse when you stroke its back and flanks as you walk behind it. Never speak unnecessarily loudly, move abruptly, or sneak up on a horse. Horses are easily spooked. A startled horse may kick or lunge before you have a chance to move out of the way. Horses can be gentle, but they are enormously powerful and they can also be dangerous. Always treat them as gently and respectfully as you want them to treat you.

You've acquainted yourself with your horse. You know its personality, and it knows yours. Now it's time to prepare your new friend for a ride.

CHAPTER 4

PREPARING FOR THE RIDE

Before you can ride, you first need to get your horse ready. Your horse should be well taken care of. This includes proper feeding and watering. It also means grooming. Then you will need to tack, or saddle and bridle, the horse.

GROOMING YOUR HORSE

If you have just fed and watered your horse, give her some time to digest. Then slide a halter over her head, hook it to a lead rope, and lead her into the barn or barnyard to groom her. Start with a hard plastic curry comb. Use quick circular motions along her neck and body to loosen the dirt and dead hair from her hide. Always move from ears to tail and never touch the delicate skin of a horse's face or legs with anything more than a cloth or soft brush. After curry-ing, take a stiff hard brush and whisk out the dirt, again from front

Grooming can be a good way for you and your horse to bond. Always be gentle so that grooming is a pleasurable experience for your horse.

to back. Then take a soft brush and smooth down her coat and legs. Comb out her mane and tail with a wide-toothed metal comb and then go over them with the soft brush.

After grooming, you will need to check your horse's feet. Stand shoulder to shoulder with her, facing her tail, and run your hand slowly and firmly down the inside of her leg. When you reach her ankle, slide your hand around her pastern (the part of the foot between the hoof and the fetlock) and press tailward until she lifts her hoof. Horses are extremely touchy about their feet and with good reason. In the center of the foot is a tender triangle of flesh called the frog that is easily irritated by stones, splinters, or careless

WHAT DOES YOUR HORSE LIKE TO EAT?

Horses are natural grazers. If they aren't getting grasses from pasture, they like to graze on hay kept nearby. They will eat a little at a time, all day long. Horses need plenty of roughage to keep their digestive tracts healthy.

Horses also like special treats. They like sweet, crunchy things such as apples, carrots, and even sugar cubes. Remember that these are special rewards and should be fed to your horse in moderation.

It is important to know that if you are feeding a horse by hand, you should keep your hand flat and your palm outstretched. If you cup your hand or feed from your fist the horse might bite you.

humans. Once you have her hoof in your hand, support it firmly. Take a hoof pick and use a gentle front to back motion along the inside of her shoe to scrape out any dirt, stones, or horse manure that may have collected there. Be very careful not to scrape the frog.

EQUIPPING YOUR HORSE

Now your horse is groomed and ready to be tacked up. Lead her to a clear area of the barn so that you can move around her easily and tie her lead rope to a hook or fence rail. When you tack up your horse, make sure you are using equipment that fits her. The saddle pad and the girth (the band that encircles the horse's waist) press directly against your horse's skin, muscle, and bone. If something rubs her, the pressure will not only be painful, it may also lower her level of trust in you. If she associates pain or discomfort with being ridden by you, she will respond less enthusiastically to your demands. Horses who have bad experiences with tacking can become difficult to saddle. They may nip, kick, buck, or run away.

SADDLING UP

To avoid aggravating your horse, check that the tree (frame) of your saddle conforms to the curve of her spine. A saddle is designed so that its tree spreads your weight over your horse's muscular back and lifts the weight off her sensitive spine. The tree needs to match the angle of her back. A saddle with a narrow tree will pinch a wide-backed horse. A wide tree will press on the withers (the ridge between the shoulders) of a narrow horse. The tree should ride clear of the withers; otherwise it may cause saddle sores. With your full weight in the saddle, you should be able to fit three fingers between your pommel (the knob at the front of the saddle) and your horse's withers.

Choosing the right saddle is essential to the success of your ride. If the saddle does not fit properly, your horse will be uncomfortable and may not trust you.

The saddle rests on a saddle pad of heavy felt that absorbs sweat and keeps moisture away from your horse's back. A saddle pad will protect your horse's skin from the leather of your saddle, but it will not compensate for a poorly fitted saddle. When you are saddling your horse, stand on her near (left) side. Be sure that she is able to see you at all times. Talk soothingly to her and tell her what you are doing. Like most of us, horses are most irritable—and most likely to bite or kick—when they are not sure what is happening.

Put your left hand on the pommel (front) and your right hand on the cantle (back) of the saddle and lift it with both hands. Make sure that the off (right) stirrup is lying over the top of the saddle so that it doesn't hit her side when you set it down on her back. Place the saddle in the concavity of her back so that it doesn't press on her withers or ride up onto her hindquarters. Settle it firmly into place and make absolutely sure that her hair is smoothed front to back beneath it. If her hair is not smooth, she will be uncomfortable and may develop saddle sores.

Your saddle is only as secure as the girth or cinch that holds it in place. Made of canvas, mohair, or more recently of high-tech neoprene, a girth needs to be both strong and comfortable against your horse's skin. When you have the saddle on, the girth will be hanging from the edge of your saddle on your horse's off (right) side. Crouch down on her near side (and run your hand down her foreleg while you do this so that she knows where you are), then reach beneath her and grab the end of the girth. Buckle it between the back of the forelegs and the swell of her belly.

You should be able to slip four fingers beneath the tightened girth and your horse's hide. Be careful not to strangle her, but be sure that your saddle won't slide off as soon as you set your foot in the stirrup. Some horses like to take a deep breath at the sight of a girth and wait until you mount to let it out. If you are not careful, you may suddenly find yourself plunging sideways around your horse's belly. If your horse uses this trick, try walking or trotting her around for a few minutes before tightening the saddle all the way. The exercise will get her heart rate up and make it harder for her to hold her breath. When she exhales, tighten the girth. When the saddle is secure, walk around to your horse's off side, touching her so she knows where you are, and let down the off stirrup.

BRIDLING

In order to bridle your horse, you must remove her halter, which is the strap you placed over her head to lead her around. It is important to hold up the bridle first, disentangle it, and prepare to slip it as swiftly and smoothly as possible over your horse's head. If you do this skillfully, she will appreciate your sureness and gain confidence in you.

Stand on your horse's near side with the bridle in one hand, neatly suspended from the brow and ear pieces. Unbuckle her halter and slide it off. Hold the bit of the bridle on the palm of your flat hand (to avoid getting your fingers nipped) and offer it to your horse's mouth while guiding the ear piece up behind her ears. If she takes the bit, slide the ear piece behind her ears, buckle the nose strap, and then buckle the throat strap. If she refuses the bit, you may be able to encourage her to open her mouth by gently pressing your thumb into the corner of her lips back behind her teeth.

Make safety a priority when choosing your riding attire. A helmet, boots, and gloves can protect you from injury.

When the bridle is fastened, the reins, which will hang in front from either side of the bit, will serve as a lead rope.

THE RIDER'S EQUIPMENT

Now that your horse is tacked and ready to go, make sure that you are as well. First, you must have a helmet. Riding can be dangerous. It is impossible to predict when a sudden scare may cause even the gentlest horse to buck and throw you, or when you might be accidentally kicked or knocked against a fence.

English riders wear black velvet hard hats or black plastic helmets with wide chinstraps and small brims. Western riders have historically worn straw or felt cowboy hats that offered no protection against a fall. Today, riding stores sell helmets that fit inside straw or felt cowboy hats, allowing you to keep the Western look while staying safe.

You may want to wear gloves. Your horse is much stronger than you are, and controlling her with leather reins or a lead rope may cause blisters or rope burns. You also need pants that allow you to move but that are not baggy. English riders tend to wear jodhpurs or breeches of snug stretch fabrics. Western riders often wear leather chaps over that most American piece of useful clothing: blue jeans.

You will need boots to give you control in the saddle and to protect your feet if your horse accidentally steps on you. Never wear sandals, and never, ever go barefoot around horses. Getting your foot stepped on (and yes, it DOES happen) hurts bad enough in sturdy, protective shoes. Bare feet can be seriously injured by a horse's hoof. English riders generally wear knee-high rubber or leather boots with breeches or short, lace-up jodhpur boots. Western riders favor the cowboy boot. Choose something strong but not too thick, and be careful to avoid soles with heavy traction such as hiking boots. A chunky sole is more likely to get caught in your stirrups, whereas a smooth-soled boot will move in and out of the stirrups more easily. This is much safer should you need to dismount in a hurry!

If you plan to ride in extreme heat or cold or in strong sunlight, dress accordingly. In the summer, wear light clothing that will not get hot in the sun. Choose loose cotton shirts, cotton breeches or jeans, sunglasses, and lots of sunblock. In the winter, wear layers of warm natural fibers like wool or toasty synthetics like polyester fleece. If you find yourself too hot at midday, you can peel off a jacket or sweater and then put it back on as the temperature drops toward evening.

Once you have your horse groomed and tacked up, and you're in your riding attire, it's time to hop on and learn how to ride!

CHAPTER 5

RIDING YOUR HORSE

*T*he first thing you will need to do is mount your horse. To do this, stand on the horse's near side and lift the reins over her head. Hold the reins in your left hand and place that hand on the pommel. Then put your right hand—your free hand—on the cantle. Place your left foot in the stirrup, push up to a standing position, and swing your right leg over the horse. Sit on the saddle and place your right foot into its stirrup.

When learning to ride, you must first learn how to feel what your body and the horse's body are doing at different speeds and gaits. Once you understand how a horse moves and how you move with it, you must learn how to use your body to direct the horse's motion. One of the best ways to accustom yourself to the feel of a horse is to ride with your eyes closed. Allow a friend or your instructor to lead your horse, then close your eyes and concentrate on the pattern of your horse's walk. At first, everything will feel

To mount your horse, place your left foot into its stirrup, hold on to the saddle, and push yourself up to a standing position. Then lower yourself onto the saddle.

strange, but quite soon you will feel improvement in your balance and in your physical reactions to your horse's motion.

SITTING IN THE SADDLE

A major factor in your ability to ride well and to control your horse is the development of a deep seat. This means sitting deep in the saddle with your back straight, your hands and heels low, your eyes forward, and your muscles alert and relaxed. Your seat is your major point of contact with your horse. If you are steady and firm in the saddle, you will move with your horse and stay put on turns,

HIGH TECH HORSEBACK RIDING

People have been riding horses for thousands of years, certainly longer than digital technology has existed. Trail riding is an activity that harkens back to a simpler time, and it requires relatively basic equipment. So how is it that technology can play a part in horseback riding?

Action cameras like GoPro can greatly enhance the sport. These cameras attach directly to your helmet and accurately record the exhilaration and beauty of a trail ride. You can show videos you've recorded on a trail ride to your friends and family and even upload them to YouTube.

In addition, you can use the Internet to find nature groups and trail riding communities. You can discuss your favorite things about horses, talk about the best trails to ride in your area, and perhaps even connect for group rides. Be sure to stay safe and never go alone when meeting someone from the Internet for the first time.

at high speeds, and over jumps. Your horse will be attuned to your presence and will sense any slight variation as a signal rather than as a random bump from a sack of potatoes.

Your instructor will have suggestions to help you find and improve your seat. Some people find it useful to pull up on the pommel with one hand and the cantle with the other and physically push themselves down into the saddle. Your instructor may

Riding bareback—without a saddle—can help you find your balance on the horse.

also improve your seat by having you ride bareback. In the beginning, riding bareback feels very insecure, but it forces you to find a true sense of balance on your horse's back.

Horses with different types of training learn to respond to different commands from their riders. For the most part, however, there are some near-universal signals that should enable you to ride most schooled horses in the United States. To walk, nudge your horse with your heels or squeeze with your calves. As she starts to move forward, think about the alignment of your body. Keep your back straight, your head up, your eyes and shoulders forward, and your hands and heels down. Keep your legs and torso still and let your hips move with your horse. Imagine that your body grows into your horse's body at the saddle like a centaur.

UNDERSTANDING YOUR HORSE'S GAIT

Your horse has four legs. This makes for much more complicated gaits than your own. Think about where each leg is when your horse walks. Learn to anticipate the rhythm of the four hooves hitting the ground. At a walk, you will have time to feel the separate motion of each leg. As your horse lifts its near hind leg, you will feel the horse's near side lift with it, lifting you and tipping you slightly forward. As the leg lands, you will descend and tilt back on the near side as you rise up on the off side. At a trot, you will feel two strong, staccato beats. At the canter, you will feel three beats: two quick bumps and a long, muscular lope.

The better your physical understanding of your horse's gaits, the better you will be able to communicate your desires to your horse. You will be able to convey your intentions to your horse through physical signals, like pressing your horse's sides with your heels or calves for speed and pulling back on the reins to slow or stop your horse. A horse can also read its rider's body language. A rider who urges a horse to speed up generally leans forward, whereas a rider who wants to stop leans back. It is important not to send mixed signals, like kicking your horse's sides while leaning back and tugging on the reins. As you improve your physical understanding

You will start out by encouraging your horse to move from a walk to a trot. You will need to learn the timing of your horse's motions. Soon you can accelerate to a canter and a gallop.

of your horse's motion, your signals and body language will grow more consistent, more effective, and subtler. When you are riding in perfect harmony with your horse, your signals will be invisible to an observer.

THE TROT, CANTER, AND GALLOP

When you want to speed up to a trot, loosen your reins, lean forward, and press your horse's sides with your legs or heels. The sitting trot is pretty bumpy. Try to absorb the motion and keep your upper body still. English riders, whose saddles are flatter than deep Western saddles, use a posting trot. Posting is an up-and-down motion timed to the bounce of a horse's trot. It allows you to take most of the shock in your flexed legs. Bear in mind that at any speed, it is dangerous to allow yourself to bump from side to side because you might bounce off.

To canter, add more pressure with your legs and wait to break out of the bouncy trot into the smooth, long thump of the canter. Keep your body straight, your hands and heels down, and your seat as deep as possible. Do not lean forward. Some horses canter so smoothly that you will feel glued into your saddle as your legs stretch down with the motion of each stride.

Past the canter is the gallop, which, although frightening at first, can be exhilarating. Be sure of your seat and your horse before you attempt to gallop. After the gallop comes the flat-out run, which is mainly appropriate for the racetrack.

After you've had some time to practice on your horse, you will feel much more comfortable. You will get to know her and she will get to know you. You may begin to develop a bond. Once you feel ready, it's time to hit the trail.

CHAPTER 6

RIDING ON THE TRAIL

You've worked hard to develop basic horse skills, and now you're ready to get out on the trail. The payoff for all this hard work and patience will be huge. You are about to embark on an activity that you can enjoy for the rest of your life. No matter where you live, you can find a place that's devoted to trail riding. Even New York City's Central Park has a horse path!

BE SENSITIVE TO YOUR HORSE

If your horse is not a seasoned trail rider, build up to serious trail work slowly. Not all horses are born trail riders. Some have trouble keeping their footing in sticky mud or on slippery rocks. If trail riding is your favorite kind of riding, you will want to keep in mind the attributes of the ideal trail horse when you are looking for a horse of your own.

The typical trail horse is extremely surefooted. She combines a long stride, a low-set head, strong bones, and wiry, adaptable muscles. She needs to be agile, intelligent, and brave. She also needs to be capable of making quick, correct decisions when picking through loose stones, navigating slick rocks, or crossing narrow ledges. If you like steep or mountainous terrain, you may prefer a horse with powerful hindquarters and large, steady hooves.

Because the trail may cover difficult terrain, make sure your horse is surefooted, strong, intelligent, and calm.

If you intend to ride in groups, you will want a horse that does not mind walking before or behind other horses. If you do find yourself on a horse that nips or kicks, you will have to ride alertly and warn anyone who comes near you of the danger. On the trail, your horse may startle easily. The first time you ride outside, your horse may spook at the sound of pine boughs, the smell of burning leaves, or the sight of a flight of monarch butterflies. Over time, she will grow accustomed to some things and you will learn which others to avoid entirely. It is important to be sensitive to your horse's fears and dislikes. Let her know that you understand and sympathize even if you have no choice but to pass the smelly rabbit farm down the road or a noisy local airfield.

STEADY AS SHE GOES

As always, when you are riding on the trail, concentrate on your seat. Ride with a loose rein. Allow your environment to help determine your speed and let your horse make footing choices without your guidance or interference. Trail riding often involves climbing and descending, which means that your horse is working harder than usual and needs your cooperation. When heading uphill, keep your weight low and steady. Do not lean on your horse's neck as this can interfere with her balance. To find the correct angle for your body on an incline, align yourself with the vertical trunks of the passing trees. Maintain your deep seat by pushing down in the stirrups. Do not hang on to the saddle, as this can add pressure to your horse's girth. If you must, grab her mane; it won't hurt her and it will stabilize you over her center.

Hold the reins loosely and trust your horse to make footing choices. Help her on inclines by angling your body in a way that helps her keep her balance.

COMPETITIVE TRAIL RIDING

If you love spending time in the wilderness and also want the challenge of competition, you should explore competitive trail riding, organized distance rides in which your goal is to cover ground more efficiently than your competitors. Some distance rides are only a few miles; others are hundreds of miles long and involve varied and unpredictable terrain. Distance riding is probably the greatest test of horse-and-rider cooperation.

Competitive trail riding is the ultimate activity for those who love trail riding and want to test themselves and their horse to the ultimate limit.

Competitive trail riding blends pleasure riding with serious horsemanship. It offers the scenery and companionship of the trail ride and demands an in-depth knowledge of trail riding skills. It also requires understanding of horse health, horse physiology, and horse psychology.

Competitive trail riding is also serious because of its length: A distance rider may be on the trail for ten days. This means both you and your horse need to be in shape and have endurance for a long haul—no small feat!

In order to train for a distance event, you will need to find terrain similar to that of the course. You will want to consider mud and water conditions, rocky or treacherous surfaces, and steepness. You will also want to think about the possibility of rain or bad weather and of extreme temperatures. You will need to start riding comparable distances in order to learn to pace yourself and learn how to pace your horse. This involves figuring out how much rest and water she needs at different temperatures and on different types of terrain. Riders beware! Sitting on a trotting horse for hours at a time can be a grueling, bumpy ride for those who are not used to it. For tricky or treacherous stretches, slow to a walk.

Competitive trail riding encompasses every element of good riding and demands high levels of communication, sympathy, and loyalty between horse and rider. When you are finally able to take your horse out on the trail for a long ride, you will experience a unique sense of accomplishment that few other recreational activities can provide.

Allow your horse to stop and rest when she needs to, and when you stop, turn sideways so that she is not standing at an angle on an incline. Riding uphill can be exhilarating; riding downhill can be terrifying. The full weight of you and your horse creates a powerful downward momentum. Your horse's neck will look dangerously far below you. Keep in mind that your horse needs your help to get down the hill safely. Do not panic, tense up, lean back, or sway from side to side. All of these things will interfere with her balance.

When you ride downhill, concentrate on centering your body and steadying your weight for your horse. Stand slightly in your stirrups so that you are barely touching the saddle and are absorbing the bumping with your legs. Keep yourself at the same angle as the passing trees. Help by watching out for particularly bad or slippery footing and lean into the opposite stirrup (on the flank opposite the foreleg that is carrying the weight) to balance her motion.

STAY CALM

Horse trainers have different approaches to helping horses learn to handle fear. Some recommend facing down a threat. Some say you should reproduce a disturbance, like the sound of a lawn mower, until it ceases to alarm your horse. Still others maintain that you should teach your horse how to ignore what you, the rider, tell her to ignore. All of these methods involve teaching your horse that the unknown is not always scary. They also stress the importance of teaching a horse to trust a rider.

Teaching a horse to behave calmly is important because an easily spooked horse poses a danger to itself, its rider, and anyone else nearby. A horse that rears or bolts can throw you or trample another animal or person. As always, it is imperative to develop a strong seat in order to hang on and exert your calm, sensible will over your panicking horse. You must always reassure your horse, and yourself, that you are in control.

Trail riding can be one of the most carefree sports. But this exhilarating activity also comes with potential hazards. Make sure you are aware of these dangers so that you can do your best to prevent them from happening. Read on to learn what to look out for.

CHAPTER 7

SAFETY FIRST

You have already learned the importance of wearing a helmet and proper attire when setting off on the trails, but there are other ways to stay safe. Since trail riding takes place in the outdoors, you should be prepared for the weather that day. You also should consider how long you'll be out.

Always go with another person or a group so that if something happens you won't be alone. It is best to go with a guide or experienced rider who knows the trails. He or she will likely bring a first aid kit and a way to contact help if you need it. And don't forget to bring a few snacks—trail riding can make you work up an appetite!

ACHES AND PAINS

When you are first learning to ride, you will be tired and sore in parts of your body you never thought could get sore–namely your

Be prepared for anything that could hamper your enjoyment of a trail ride, such as strong sun, high temperatures, and minor injuries.

rear and the insides of your legs. If you push yourself too hard, you may strain a muscle or tendon or sprain a ligament. It is important to learn some basic first aid rules (such as RICE: Rest, Ice, Compression, and Elevation for strains and sprains) and to make a point of carrying bandages and antibiotic ointment for minor cuts and scrapes.

THE ELEMENTS

All outdoor sports put you at risk of sun damage. Always wear a riding helmet with a brim, as well as sunglasses and sunblock. In addi-

OVERCOMING ANXIETY

Riding a horse can be difficult for new riders. It's so much more complicated than riding a bicycle because it involves sitting atop a living, breathing creature with its own mind and emotions. But anxiety can also cripple seasoned riders who have had a bad experience like a fall. For these people, who suffer from post-traumatic fear, even being inside a stable can bring forth tears and feelings of loss of control.

The best way to deal with post-traumatic fear is to enlist the help of one or several professionals. They can ease you back into the saddle by using the most important quality: patience. It may be that you will start by just looking at a horse. Then you might feel comfortable patting or grooming the horse. After much exposure to the horse, the professionals can help you mount and ride the horse. You will need to work on understanding your anxiety and developing tools to cope with it. It won't be fast or easy, but you learn to keep fear from hampering your enjoyment of trail riding.

tion, be aware that heat stress can lead to fatigue, exhaustion, errors in judgment, and eventually heatstroke. On a hot day, a serious ride may drain you of a gallon of fluid every hour. Minor heat stress can cause headaches, a quickened pulse, and fatigue. If you feel any of these symptoms, rest in the shade and drink water until you feel normal. More serious heat stress will make you pale, sweaty, weak, and nauseated. Severe heat stress can trigger heatstroke. Victims of severe heat stress look hot and flushed. Their temperatures rise, they breathe rapidly, and they stop sweating. They need immediate medical help.

Heat is not the only outdoor danger. Cold or damp weather can interfere with your circulation. In extreme circumstances, it can cause frostbite. In a sudden snow or rainstorm, you may run the risk of hypothermia, a state in which your body temperature drops to dangerous levels. Hypothermia is made worse by hunger and fatigue and needs to be treated by a doctor.

Riding on a trail of freshly fallen snow can be a great experience, but you won't enjoy it if you are freezing. Dress properly, and avoid the trail if temperatures are too low.

Once you have tried trail riding a few times, you might want to learn about other kinds of horseback riding, including jumping and dressage.

ALTITUDE

The air at high mountain altitudes is thinner than air at sea level. This means that it provides less oxygen to you and your horse. This can make you feel dizzy and weak. It can also affect your judgment. If you plan a trail riding trip in higher or more mountainous terrain than where you and your horse live, make sure that you take a day or two for both of your systems to adjust to the higher altitude before you undertake any strenuous riding.

While trail riding can pose certain dangers, being prepared will help you solve problems if they come up. The more experience you have, the better prepared you'll be. There are a lot of things to consider when you embark on a trail ride, but don't let that get in the way of your enjoyment. There are few things in life that combine exercise, an appreciation of nature, and bonding with animals as successfully as trail riding.

GLOSSARY

APPALOOSA A breed of horse distinguishable by its spotted coat. The Appaloosa is an American breed.

ARABIAN An ancient North African breed of horse distinguishable by its conformation, its stamina, its intelligence, and its spirited temperament.

DISHED FACE A phrase used to describe a feature of a horse's conformation in which the profile of the face looks slightly concave; usually a sign of Arabian breeding.

DRESSAGE A style of competitive riding that emphasizes precision maneuvers and control of the horse by imperceptible commands.

FOAL A baby horse less than one year old.

FROG The triangle of sensitive flesh in a horse's hoof.

HAND A length of four inches. A horse's height is measured in hands from the ground up to the shoulder.

HERD A community of grazing animals, such as horses or cows. Herd animals are social in nature and tend to be easily guided by a dominant member of the herd or a human master.

INTERBREEDING Mating two different breeds of horses to produce a foal with the traits of both parents.

PAINT A breed of horse distinguishable by its splotchy coat that resembles a paint-splattered surface. The paint is an American breed.

PALOMINO A breed of horse distinguishable by its tawny golden body and white mane and tail. The palomino is an American breed.

SEAT How a rider sits in the saddle. A secure seat is the mark of a capable rider.

SPOOK To startle a horse with a loud noise or sudden movement.

STALLION An ungelded male horse. Stallions are usually larger, more muscular, and higher spirited than mares or geldings of the same breed. Only experienced riders and handlers should work with stallions.

SUREFOOTED The ability to travel smoothly and safely on rocky, slippery, or difficult terrain.

TACK Riding gear worn by horses, such as saddles and bridles.

FOR MORE INFORMATION

American Association for Horsemanship Safety
4125 Fish Creek Road
Estes Park, CO 80517
(866) 485-6800
Website: http://www.horsemanshipsafety.com
The American Association for Horsemanship Safety is dedicated to teaching and enforcing safe methods of horseback instruction.

American Competitive Trail Horse Association
637 Soda Creek Road
Spicewood, TX 78669
(877) 992-2842
Website: https://www.actha.us/
ACTHA organizes and finds sponsors for rides all across the United States. ACTHA is also committed to horse rescue and easing the suffering of horses in need.

American Quarter Horse Association
1600 Quarter Horse Drive
Amarillo, TX 79104
(806) 376-4811
Website: http://www.aqha.com
The American Quarter Horse Association is the world's largest equine breed registry and membership organization. Members will be alerted to competitions around the country and will receive the association's trade journal.

American Riding Instructors Association
28801 Trenton Court
Bonita Springs, FL 34134-3337
Website: https://www.riding-instructor.com
The American Riding Instructors Association promotes excellence in the profession of horseback riding instruction, based on the principles of safety, knowledge, and integrity, with the health, happiness, and well-being of studnts and horses being of primary concern.

FOR MORE INFORMATION

Equine Canada
308 Legget Drive, Suite 100
Ottawa Ontario K2K 1Y6
Canada
(866) 282-8395
Website: http://equinecanada.ca
From championing best practices to encouraging fun and participation, Equine Canada is a dedicated national voice working to serve, promote, and protect the interests of horses and Canada's equestrian community.

Ontario Trail Riders Association
P.O. Box 3038
Elmvale, ON
Canada L0L 1P0
Website: http://www.otra.ca/
OTRA's mission is to promote recreational trail riding and the creation, development, preservation, and safe use of trails. Over the years OTRA has strived to achieve these goals by initiating many large projects to draw attention to the need for more trails for equestrians. OTRA has members representing the equestrian interest on rail trail development committees, regional forest management committees, and local trail groups.

United States Equestrian Federation
4047 Iron Works Parkway
Lexington, KY 40511
(859) 258 2472
Website: https://www.usef.org/
The USEF is dedicated to uniting the equestrian community, honoring achievement, and serving as guardians of equestrian sport. Since its inception in 1917, the federation has been dedicated to pursuing excellence and promoting growth, all while providing and maintaining a safe and level playing field for both its equine and human athletes.

WEBSITES

Because of the changing nature of Internet links, Rosen Publishing has developed an online list of websites related to the subject of this book. This site is updated regularly. Please use this link to access this list:

http://www.rosenlinks.com/OUT/Trail

FOR FURTHER READING

Bolender, Mark. *Bolender's Guide to Mastering Mountain and Extreme Trail Riding*. Bloomington, IN: Iuniverse, 2012.

Bratten, Donna Bowman. *From Head to Tail: All About Horse Care*. North Mankato, MN: Capstone Press, 2014.

Carlson, Jack and Elizabeth Stewart. *Superstition Wilderness Trails West: Hikes, Horse Rides, and History*. Tempe, AZ: Clear Creek Pub., 2012.

Collins, Lindsay G. *The Trail Riders' Handbook*. Maryborough, Australia: Lindsay G. Collins, 2012.

Fitzpatrick, Andrea. *The Ultimate Guide to Horse Breeds*. Edison, NJ: Chartwell Books, 2014.

Goodnight, Julie and Heidi Nyland Melocco. *Goodnight's Guide to Great Trail Riding: A How-to for You and Your Horse*. Boulder, CO: Equine Network, 2011.

Hayes, Tim. *Riding Home: The Power of Horses to Heal*. New York, NY: St. Martin's Press, 2015.

Hicks, Charlie. *Horseback Riding: The Complete Beginner's Guide*. Papillion, NE: Horse Training Resources, 2012.

Jeffrey, Laura S. *Choosing a Horse: How to Choose and Care for a Horse*. Berkeley Heights, NJ: Enslow Publishers, 2013.

Kissock, Heather. *Horseback Riding*. New York, NY: AV2 by Weigl, 2014.

Myers, Micaela. *Trail Riding*. Irvine, CA: I-5 Publishing, 2014.

Roome, Pippa and Catherine Austen. *Choosing & Looking After Your Horse*. London, England: Flame Tree, 2014.

Stamps, Caroline. *Horseback Riding: A Step-by-Step Guide to the Secrets of Horseback Riding*. New York, NY: DK Publishing, 2012.

Stamps, Caroline. *Horses*. New York, NY: DK Publishing, 2014.

Vogel, Colin. *Complete Horse Care Manual*. London, England: Dorling Kindersley, 2011.

INDEX

S

saddling, 28–31
Shetland ponies, 17–18
sleep, 22

T

thoroughbreds, 12, 16–17
trail riding
     competitive, 46–47
     pacing, 43–44
     sitting, 44, 48
trotting, 40–41
trust, 48–49

W

Welsh mountain ponies, 18–19

ABOUT THE AUTHORS

Viola Jones is a writer and middle school teacher who grew up helping her grandfather groom the horses on his farm.

Allison Stark Draper is a writer and editor. She lives in New York City and the Catskills.

PHOTO CREDITS

Cover, p. 1 Iakov Filimonov/Shutterstock.com; p. 5 Noel Hendrickson/ Digital Vision/Getty Images; p. 7 Richard T. Nowitz/Science Source; p. 8 DEA/G. Nimatallah/De Agostini/Getty Images; p. 11 Don Cook/ Moment Open/Getty Images; p. 15 Mary981/iStock/Thinkstock; p. 18 Kevin Schafer/Digital Vision/Getty Images; p. 21 auremar/Shutterstock. com; p. 23 iLight photo/Shutterstock.com; p. 26 Lumi Images/Alexandra Dost/Getty Images; pp. 28-29 Cultura RM/Henglein and Steets/ Getty Images; p. 32 YanLev/iStock/Thinkstock; p. 36 Val Loh/The Image Bank/Getty Images; p. 38 Shotgun/Shutterstock.com; p. 40 My Good Images/Shutterstock.com; pp. 42-43 Bill Gruber/Shutterstock.com; p. 45 JordiDelgado/iStock/Thinkstock; p. 46 Rick Hyman/E+/Getty Images; p. 51 Peter Wollinga/Shutterstock.com; p. 53 Lenkadan/Shutterstock. com; pp. 54-55 by ana_gr/Moment Open/Getty Images; cover and interior pages Iwona Grodzka/iStock/Thinkstock (twig frame), AKIRA/ amanaimagesRF/Thinkstock (wood frame)
Designer: Brian Garvey; Editor: Christine Poolos
Photo researcher: Carina Finn